Hershey Children's Garden

at Cleveland Botanical Garden

Hershey Children's Garden

A Place to Grow

Maureen Heffernan

Ohio University Press, Athens

IN ASSOCIATION WITH

Cleveland Botanical Garden

Ohio University Press, Athens, Ohio 45701

© 2004 by Ohio University Press

Printed in China

All rights reserved

Ohio University Press books are printed on acid-free paper ∞ ™

12 11 10 09 08 07 06 05 04   5 4 3 2 1

Library of Congress Cataloging-in-Publication Data
Heffernan, Maureen.
    Hershey Children's Garden : a place to grow / Maureen Heffernan.
        p. cm.
      ISBN 0-8214-1583-2 (pbk. : alk. paper)
    1. Hershey Children's Garden (Cleveland, Ohio) 2. Children's gardens. I. Title.
      SB466U7H44 2004
      635—dc22

                                    2004008191

This book is dedicated to Debra Hershey Guren and her family.

Debra Hershey Guren helping
young visitors learn in the
Hershey Children's Garden at
Cleveland Botanical Garden.

Sprinkling Stars

I went to the Garden
one sunny day
And soon it started
to rain

So I walked back
up to the pond

And sat undernearth
a Willow tree

I looked out at the pond
And said it looked
like sprinkling stars!

written by Caroline Gray, eight years old,
after visiting the Hershey Children's Garden
at Cleveland Botanical Garden

Contents

Foreword

THERE ARE GOOD REASONS THIS BOOK IS DEDICATED TO Debra Hershey Guren and her family. Debbie's intuitive understanding of how children experience their environment had a profound impact on the design of the garden. Debbie's own childhood experiences exploring both fields and gardens, her education as a school psychologist, and her longstanding involvement with Montessori education made her a uniquely qualified member of the garden's design team. Even now, she continues to volunteer in the garden every week. The Hershey family's generous support and commitment made it possible for the garden to become a reality. Hershey Children's Garden honors the memory of Debra Hershey Guren's parents, Jo and Alvin.

This was a dream project. The design team of Debra Guren, Herb Schaal of the landscape architecture firm EDAW Inc., and Cleveland Botanical Garden's Maureen Heffernan brought incredible creativity and a child-first attitude to planning the garden that was exhilarating to everyone involved. The plan that they created was both fantastical and natural. Pete Baumgarten of Donley's Inc. and Jeff Knopf of Behnke Associates in turn led a team of artists and artisans who made the fantasy a reality.

In the years since the garden opened, plants have grown and the structures have acquired the patina of thousands of little hands exploring, playing, learning, and making joyous memories. Hershey Children's Garden has become an integral part of the lives of a generation of children. Perhaps the greatest kudos comes from my grandson Sam, who says it is the best place in the world to play hide-and-seek with his grandpa.

Brian Holley
Director
Cleveland Botanical Garden

Introduction

I HAD THE GREAT GOOD LUCK to grow up in the country on a farm. My brother and sisters and I had the run of our farm and grew up entirely outdoors, playing in our fields, vineyards, woods, and along the banks of a creek where, sitting on its railroad-tie bridge, we passed hot summer days dangling our feet in its slow current of muddy but cool water.

When I think back to our farm, one image that always comes to mind is the long rows of Concord grapes my grandfather had planted. In early fall, you could sniff the air and know if the grapes were ripe. It was a thrill to discover a cluster of ripe, juicy grapes hiding under the leaves and to pick them at will to pop into your mouth.

Another vivid memory is of when I was about seven years old, and my mother helped us plant our first garden. She helped us clear a small bit of an open field, and my brother and sister and I planted corn and marigold seeds, and onion and tomato starts. We filled buckets with water from an old, rusty pump behind a shed and watered the seeds and plants every day.

Before too long, delicate lines of tender green corn and flower shoots appeared. We watered and weeded, and by high summer we had corn taller then we were, sweet ripe tomatoes we picked and ate right in the garden, and yellow marigolds. We played in the corn rows, and I remember feeling proud and protective of our little vegetable garden. The corn and tomatoes seemed to take on an awesome magical quality. The soft corn silk felt like our pet rabbit's ears. A few weeks later, we were picking endless ears of corn from our little corn patch.

The author (*right*) in her garden as a child, with siblings Anne and John.

These experiences gave me a reverence for plants, gardens, farms, and the outdoors. Nature revealed her everyday miracles of a flower blooming, a grape cluster ripening, leaves turning color, a rose's fragrance, the sound of frogs plopping into a creek, dragonflies buzzing, clouds changing shape against a deep blue sky and the smell of mown hay and plowed fields after a rain as the soil released its scent like spring incense. As the quotation from Luther Burbank states at the garden's entrance, these experiences were the best part of my childhood education.

When you understand how these experiences shape you, you realize how good it is for all children to have experiences of the same kind.

Hershey Children's Garden was created to offer garden and nature discoveries and experiences for children that they will remember fondly all their lives.

Like the world of *The Secret Garden,* this garden offers children, especially children growing up in urban areas, a glimpse into a thrilling world that may have been hidden from them.

Everyone involved in developing the Hershey Children's Garden felt privileged and happy to be creating a place that could ignite or deepen a child's love and appreciation for nature.

We hope that, when the children who come to our garden grow up, they in turn will be motivated to make and tend gardens and to help preserve natural areas in their corner of the world.

A lot of love went into making this garden, and I think visitors can see and feel it when they enter. Please come for a visit.

A Garden Grows

Children's Gardens Begin to Grow

A HORTICULTURAL REVOLUTION HAS GENTLY SWEPT across the country since the early 1990s. Since that time, a number of major new public children's gardens have opened throughout the country, and many more are currently being constructed or planned.

Visitor surveys show that often up to half of all visitors to botanical gardens are children. The "lightbulb" idea behind all these new children's gardens was, Why ignore half your audience? Most children are not thrilled by regular public gardens. Although adults find them beautiful and interesting, most children become bored and restless just strolling past tastefully maintained beds and borders.

However, if a garden is created with child-sized structures, secret spaces, interactive features, fun theme plantings, big bright flowers, and water, it will attract and hold the interest of children for hours—even have them crying when parents say it's time to go.

Designed to lure children off the beaten garden path, the

We wanted a
garden filled
with natural
discoveries—
like the chance
to study
a praying
mantis or . . .

. . . find
secret places.

new children's gardens usher them into exuberant, playful spaces that capture their imaginations with natural discoveries and secret places. Igniting children's interest in plants and gardening when they are young can help spark a lifelong love of plants and gardening. As the English garden writer Gertrude Jekyll said, "The love of gardening is a seed that once sown never dies."

Children's gardens are gardens of joy—gardens that tickle our hearts and mind with childlike, effervescent energy, wonder, and delight. They contain simple yet profound experiences and spaces that speak deeply to children and to the "inner child" of grown-ups.

Immediately upon entering Hershey Children's Garden, visitors are moved by the Luther Burbank quotation, charmed by the butterfly gate, amused by toddlers playing in the bubbling sun fountain and blowing winds, and entertained by the baby scarecrows doing somersaults on a cottage wildflower roof. And that's just the entrance . . .

2

That children need to have contact and meaningful experiences with plants and gardens is not a new concept. However, because more and more of today's children have little daily contact with nature, the sense of urgency to provide places where children can discover plants, gardens, and nature in playful and educational ways has provided further fuel to this movement.

A Children's Garden Grows in Cleveland

In 1994, as trustees of Cleveland Botanical Garden discussed a children's garden to be created in an undeveloped area of Cleveland Botanical Garden, trustee Debra Hershey Guren mentioned to the Garden's director that she could possibly further help with the idea.

Debra, a Montessori education advocate, inherited her love of gardening and education from her mother, Jo Hershey Selden. Before Mrs. Selden died in 1990, she set up a Charitable Remainder Trust that named Cleveland Botanical Garden as one of its beneficiaries. When Debra and her siblings notified the Garden of the gift at that time, they were told about the idea to create a learning garden and they agreed that their mother would have liked the money to go toward such a garden. As plans for a learning garden evolved into plans for a children's garden, Jo Hershey Selden's gift became the seed money to fund the children's garden.

Thanks to the Hershey family's successful insurance business, Jo Hershey Selden had also been able to establish a philanthropic foundation, The Hershey Foundation, which is dedicated to providing northeast Ohio children from all socioeconomic and cultural backgrounds with special opportunities for personal growth and development.

Debra and her siblings, who now manage the foundation, decided that the kind of children's garden being discussed exactly fit the foundation's mission and would be a loving tribute to her parents—especially to her mother's love of gardens.

When The Hershey Foundation, along with Hershey family members, pledged additional funds to create a new children's garden, the seed for the garden germinated and quickly started to grow.

The Intent of the Garden

Having the funds in place, a committee of trustees, staff, and invited garden design and horticultural experts began planning the garden.

Our first task was figuring out what kind of children's garden to create. With infinite ways to go, we fortunately reached a consensus at our first meeting: "No Disney!"

"No Disney" was the motto. No plastic, no gimmicks, no "too cute," no con-

trived, no overly designed, manicured, or inauthentic spaces. We did not want
an outdoor museum where kids press a buzzer and quickly move on to the next
buzzer.

We thought about the outdoor places we had loved as children. As members of
our group shared memories, we realized there were many similarities—most of us
had a favorite tree we loved to climb to hide from the world for a while; we loved
climbing rock piles and picking corn, strawberries, and apples. We all made forts
in woods with old blankets, boxes, and branches, or explored vacant lots; we built
rickety treehouses, dug for worms, and most especially loved any place with water—
creeks, ponds, pools, or puddles.

Feeding these experiences into the design process, we realized we wanted a
garden that is a little wild around the edges, with natural, uncultivated areas for
children to explore. We wanted a *Secret Garden* garden, in which every nook and
cranny reveals a wonderful natural or artistic surprise.

We wanted a garden where all the senses merrily compete for attention in an
atmosphere of magical realism . . . we wanted kids to murmur "wow" when they
taste a chocolate mint leaf, to smell lemon verbena, to splash in a fountain, to feel
grasses tickle them as they walk along a path and hear frogs jumping and croaking,
and to see a dazzling rainbow of flower colors.

In addition, we wanted the garden to be packed with teachable moments so
children can see where food comes from, how a seed forms and germinates, how
roots grow, how the parts of a flower function, how worms help plants, and
nature's many fascinating interconnections.

In other words, we wanted a childhood Eden that also inspires learning, curios-
ity, and a love of plants and nature in children. The task of transforming an
unremarkable half-acre or so of land into an Eden
would require an exceptional designer. After an inten-
sive national search, Herb Schaal was hired as the
project's landscape architect, bringing to the project
his award-winning design skills and a special interest
and experience in designing children's gardens.

HERB SCHAAL has received more than forty-five national, state, regional, and local awards for his innovative landscape design work. He is a principal with the landscape architecture firm EDAW Inc. at its Fort Collins, Colorado, office and is a fellow in the American Society of Landscape Architects.

He has worked for more than twenty public gardens and fifty public parks. His interactive designs include children's gardens for the Gateway Science School and Children's Hospital, both in St. Louis, and for Red Butte Garden in Salt Lake City, as well as the therapy garden at Denver Botanic Garden.

He has completed plans for a number of new children's gardens to be created at the Lewis Ginter Botanical Garden in Richmond, Virginia; the Lena Meijer Children's Garden at the Frederik Meijer Gardens and Sculpture Park in Grand Rapids, Michigan; and the Quad City Botanical Center in Rock Island, Illinois.

Children drew pictures of what they wanted to have in a garden.

What Do Children Want?

As part of the design process, we invited children to come to Cleveland Botanical Garden one evening and tell us what they wanted to have in a garden. We rolled

out paper on the floor and armed kids with crayons. Getting right to work, dozens of children quickly created vivid crayon tapestries of trees, flowers, birds, butterflies, apples, picket fences, treehouses, squirrels, watermelons, grapes, strawberries, tomatoes, corn, grass, clouds, suns, ponds, and waterfalls along with many indecipherable objects of desire.

Can you guess what item most kids drew? Apple trees were the number one item, followed by flowers, treehouses, ponds, birds, and cornstalks.

6

And More Ideas . . .

Project committee members studied
their favorite garden design books
for ideas. Three books were especially
inspiring: *Family Gardens* by Bunny
Guinness, the classic *Children and Gardens*
by Gertrude Jekyll, and *A Child's Garden* by
Molly Dannenmaier.

The Finished Design

In early spring of 1998, the garden
design was finished. It divided the
garden into two major areas—a natural
woodland and a cultivated garden area—
with a grand entrance area featuring a
fountain court.

A treehouse, pond, bridge, bird
blind, and rock-climbing wall highlighted the shady native plant woodland. A
child's cottage, a prairie meadow, a vegetable and fruit garden, an International
Garden, an evergreen maze, and a recycled container garden rounded out the
sunny cultivated garden area.

Thanks to Herb Schaal and our collaboration with him, the design met our
aspirations for a place of beauty and discovery consisting of equal parts wildness
and cultivation topped off with unlimited opportunities for education and play.

CLEVELAND BOTANICAL GARDEN

HERSHEY CHILDREN'S GARDEN

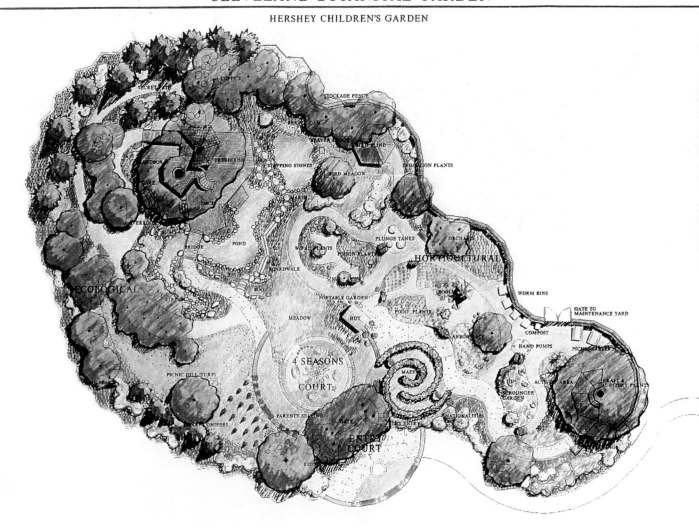

SITE PLAN

EDAW

0   5   10   20

Hershey Children's Garden master plan drawing.

Groundbreaking

On June 1, 1998, a brilliant sunny day nearly ten months after the start of our planning process, a groundbreaking celebration was held. Debra Hershey Guren spoke of her parents, especially of her mother's love of gardening and fondness for Cleveland Botanical Garden, which inspired her family's philanthropic decision to fund the project.

The children's garden will be an ideal place to learn about the environment, the process by which seeds become food, the interconnectedness of nature, and the importance of nurturing and caring for living things. The children's garden will be a special place to play in and learn from, to imagine and experience. . . . This project was a natural to fund, a perfect fit, combining education, children, and gardening, all of my mother's passions.

We had created an exciting design—at least on paper.
Now, it was time to roll in the heavy equipment and bring the plan to life.

Constructing the Garden

Donley's Inc., a Cleveland construction firm, was selected to build the garden. Construction began in July 1998 and was completed in early June 1999. The first task was clearing the garden area of about a dozen trees to create sunny areas as well as to eliminate safety hazards posed by diseased or older, weak trees. Several tree trunks were saved to create log tables and chairs for the garden.

Left to right: Loren Hershey, Ruth Eppig, Debra Hershey Guren, Brian Holley, and Carole Hershey Walters take the first shovelfuls, after which the Hershey family's children and grandchildren join in the digging.

9

The next large task was building the stream and pond. As soil was excavated, it was used to build up a gently sloping bank behind the treehouse area climbing wall.

Once digging was completed, concrete was poured to create the stream and pond and was also shaped into naturalistic boulders to line the stream and pond edges.

The unused woodland area where the children's garden was to be built.

Building the pond area and treehouse.

Installing bronze art pieces into the Four Season's Court.

Overlooking the pond, a deck and treehouse were built around two large tulip trees, with care taken not to damage the trees' roots.

Once the pond was well along, construction began on the Four Seasons Fountain Court. Its sun fountain, blowing wind faces, and sundial challenged the construction crew to ensure all the parts worked correctly.

Workers carefully drilled a narrow passage through each wind boulder to insert plastic tubing that would connect to a water line to allow the winds to "blow" mist from the wind faces' mouths.

Before the sundial pieces were set, the construction team had to ensure they were exactly positioned to face magnetic north and "set" to daylight saving time so the sundial reading matches clock time from spring through fall.

Garden Pathways

Everywhere visitors look in Hershey Children's Garden, they see charming details. But how do you make concrete pathways charming? We decided to turn our concrete pathways into a wildlife interstate with squirrel, deer, beaver, duck, fox, frog, rabbit, blue heron, raccoon, bear, and eagle tracks.

Using a variety of rubber animal tracks ordered from a catalog, on the day the concrete pathways were poured, we set down tracks of a sly red fox sneaking up on a rabbit; a mama duck and her ducklings crossing the pathway headed for a swim in the pond; deer trying to get into the vegetable garden; a squirrel scampering toward an oak tree's delicious acorns; and a bear who just caught a tasty fish near the pond.

Garden Artists and Craftspeople

In an overly franchised, mass-merchandise world, we wanted a garden with a unique sense of place. To accomplish this, we engaged artists and craftspeople to create one-of-a-kind garden artwork and structures.

With the assistance of Cleveland Public Art, we discovered the work of Cleveland area artists Mary Wawyrtko, who created the fountain court pieces, and Brinsley Tyrell, who

Maureen Heffernan and Young-Mi Moon planning animal track patterns for the sidewalks.

11

Mary Wawyrtko's bronze sun fountain.

designed the entry gates. Both artists brought expert design skills and a whimsical storybook sensibility to the project.

Mary Wawyrtko created the Four Seasons Fountain Court artwork, including the sun fountain face, wind faces, comets, stars, elfin leap year figure, Luther Burbank medallion, and Cotton Candy, the garden's bronze pony sculpture.

Brinsley Tyrell, a professor of design at

Mary Wawyrtko collaborated with Campbell Paxton, a Cleveland artist specializing in mythological bronze sculptures, to create the Four Winds faces.

Stone carver Lothar Jobczyk designed and carved seasonal motifs on each boulder. For the winter/north wind, observant visitors can find several perfect snowflakes. Look also for spring's rain cloud and lightning bolt; summer's bird and butterfly; and falling leaves on the autumn boulder.

Kent State University who has gar-
nered numerous commissions for
large public art projects, created the
garden's main entry gates and two
gate entrances just for children.

Brinsley's magnificent butterfly
gates are alive with a circus of insects
including grasshoppers, beetles,
slugs, bees, ladybugs, and snails
happily crawling on leaves and
flowers. Equally charming are the
child-sized insect gates with beetles
and a large praying mantis.

Brinsley collaborated with Steve
Toudau, an ironworker from Cleve-
land, who fabricated the gates at the
Rose Iron Works in Cleveland.

David Robinson, from Trenton, New Jersey,
designed and built the garden's treehouse, pond
bridge, toolshed, and bird blind. His company,
Natural Edge, specializes in using cedar logs
and branches in their natural form to build free-
form-style structures. His work can also be seen in
Central Park's Children's Zoo, Camden Children's
Garden, and the New York Botanical Garden.
David's meticulous planning and construction
techniques ensure these structures will be enjoyed
by several generations.

One of two
child-only
entry gates
created by
Brinsley
Tyrell.

David
Robinson's
whimsical
treehouse.

Everything in the children's garden, from doorways to trellises and brooms, is child-sized.

Child-Sizing the Garden: Not Too Big, Not Too Small, Just Right!

A big part of getting the garden right is child-sizing it. We made sure all the gate and door handles, hand pumps, stepping-stones, bird blind peepholes, arbors, seating, wind faces, rock-climbing wall, and cottage are child-, not adult-, sized.

Compost bins were designed with easily removable front slats so children can help us compost. In the Scrounger's Garden, shoes, teapots, and football helmets are set on or low to the ground so even toddlers can easily pour water over them.

Plant Selection

Once the hardscapes and structures were completed in early spring, it was finally time to turn the space into a garden.

Working from Herb Schaal's plant placement plan, we selected woodland and garden plants following a set of general guidelines. We aimed to choose plants that

1. interest and delight children;
2. ensure maximum color, fragrance, and interest from early spring through fall when the garden would be open;
3. include as many native plants as possible;
4. are hardy and drought-tolerant; and
5. come from local nurseries.

Walking along the entry border, visitors stop in their tracks when they see the dinner plate–size moon-white swamp mallow hibiscus.

Beds and Borders

In the sunny, cultivated theme garden areas, the plan is to have spring-to-fall color and interest in every nook and cranny and to create a storybook or cottage garden style.

We do not want the garden to look too professionally perfect and thus risk losing the special feeling of informality, magic, and enchantment we are after. Therefore, plants are purposely exuberant in height and color, like the towering mondo grasses and Joe-Pye weed; the brilliantly dark-purple 'Dartmoor' butterfly bushes, and the scarlet wooly cockscomb.

Plants are a bit crowded to show off unexpected juxtapositions—like a giant sunflower growing up through a shrub rose, or candy-cane petunias growing around hot yellow primroses.

Garden Docents

From early in the garden planning process, we knew we wanted people, not signs, to teach kids about plants and gardening. We recruit and train volunteers to be friendly, knowledgeable figures in the garden. Our devoted garden docents, in bright bee-yellow smocks, may be catching monarch butterflies to show kids, potting up bean seeds to teach children about germination, or inviting little visitors to plant a daffodil bulb or learn the name of a flower.

Our garden docents welcome children and invite them to see or learn new things on each visit.

Planting

Planting began in early April 1999 and continued seemingly nonstop right up through those last few colorful Scrounger's containers the morning of the official opening.

Trees and shrubs were planted first, followed by the perennials and annuals. The garden seemed to swallow truckload after truckload of plants in giant gulps. Original plant estimates were revised upward, resulting in many trips to area nurseries and garden centers to find "just a few" more plants, which yielded unexpected new planting ideas. Planting plans got set aside and "field placement"

ruled the day. In garden design, it's a good thing to be open to a design change when inspiration or luck strikes.

One of our best unexpected finds was at Losely Nursery in Perry, Ohio. Out in their growing fields to select a hemlock tree, we spotted two deciduous larch trees that had formed a perfect arch. Snatching them up, we brought them right back and planted them at one of the woodland entry areas to create an enchanting, silky, green Larch Arch that visitors love.

So kids can learn plant names, we wanted to label a good number of plants. However, we did not want regular, uniform labels that would detract from the garden's charm. Our solution was to invite a Girl Scout troop to paint pictures of the plants and write their names on small wooden labels. This practice continues each year with different youth groups, with the result that each label is a charming, one-of-a-kind work of art.

All the garden's plant labels are painted by children.

The garden's famous Larch Arch creates a soft, fringy threshold to walk under in the woodland garden.

Watering and Waiting

Despite an exceptionally hot and dry spring and early summer in 1999, plants were growing and thriving, thanks to much watering and mulching.

The finished garden was indeed beautiful, magical, charming, and filled with wonders.

All it needed to make it a children's garden was just one more thing—children.

Opening Day—June 27, 1999

After nearly two years of planning, building, and planting, it was opening day. Suddenly, it was a true children's garden with laughter, smiles, and shouts as children went about the work and play of investigating all the pieces and parts of the garden—especially the watery ones on that very hot day. Kids jumped into the stream, dangled their legs in the pond, and got happily soaked in the fountain.

The pond was officially christened that day by having children release three large bullfrogs into its water lily–covered waters.

Debra Hershey Guren, along with her brothers, Barry (left) and Loren (right), and the Garden's director, Brian Holley, cut the ribbon, allowing scores of children to stream into the garden.

A Tour of the Garden

WALKING OUT TOWARD THE CHILDREN'S GARDEN, visitors begin to notice that something special is starting to happen, that they're "not in Kansas anymore" but haven fallen into a place of magical realism. Along the walkway, a jubilant flower border with waves of rich color and fragrance acts like a gentle current drawing visitors up to the entrance of the garden.

Designed as a butterfly garden with a cottage garden style, the entry border charms visitors with its unbridled exuberance from spring through fall. In spring, a dazzling display of daffodils, tulips, and hyacinths gives way to early summer's brilliant theatrics of foxgloves, peonies, roses, alliums, astilbes, and lavender, which eventually relinquish the spotlight to high summer's purple butterfly bushes, butterfly weed, black-eyed Susan, catmint, coneflowers, and hibiscus. The towering purple butterfly bushes and butterfly weed attract scores of butterflies that seem to flutter down onto the border like nature's confetti.

As summer wanes, fall's fireworks shoot up with breathtaking displays of

Like Dorothy landing in Oz, visitors to the Hershey Children's Garden feel as if they too have fallen into a magical place.

asters, Japanese anemones, rich red pineapple sage, glowing solidagoes, and Joe-Pye weed, the gentle giant with the lavender rose flowers, towering over all.

Our butterfly border is not all grown-up and well behaved. Its sunflowers grow through rosebushes between a banana tree and a yellow butterfly bush. Kids and adults stop and touch the lamb's ears and follow the flutterings of swallowtail and monarch butterflies that flock to the border.

Luther Burbank Quotation

Just outside the garden entry, set into the paving stones, is a clay medallion with a chiseled quote from the plantsman Luther Burbank that beautifully communicates to visitors what this garden is all about.

Every child should have mud pies, grasshoppers, water bugs, tadpoles, frogs, mud turtles, elderberries, wild strawberries, acorns, chestnuts, trees to climb, brooks to wade, water lilies, woodchucks, bats, bees, butterflies, various animals to pet, hayfields, pine-cones, rocks to roll, sand, snakes,

huckleberries and hornets; and any child who has been deprived of these has been deprived of the best part of his education.

—Luther Burbank, 1929

The Luther Burbank quotation is framed by little hands. Look closely for a red fox who also endorses the quote with a paw.

Close-up of
busy ants and
a beetle on the
butterfly gates.

Butterfly Gates

Looking up from the Burbank plaque, visitors see the garden's
signature butterfly and insect gates framed by two little-leaf
linden trees and "kids-only" insect gates. On each visit to
the garden, visitors seem to discover a new leaf, flower, or
one of the snails, ants, beetles, praying mantises, flies,
wasps, bees, and wooly caterpillars that make up the gates.

By lifting the arm of a praying mantis, on the left
gate, or a beetle, on the right, kids open the gates and
walk through a grapevine tunnel to enter the garden.
In the fall, they can pick delicious Concord grapes
from inside the tunnel.

21

Four Seasons Fountain Court

The Four Seasons Fountain Court greets visitors as they enter the garden. Meant
to draw down the celestial visually
into the garden, it communicates
how the four seasons in a garden
are linked to the earth's journey
around the sun and how the
phases of the moon also effect
changes on the earth. Spring,
summer, fall, and winter arrive
and depart as the earth moves
around the sun. A sun fountain in
the court's center symbolizes how
water and light are crucial for
plants to grow and indeed for all
life to flourish.

**There is no
better place to
cool down on
hot days than
in the sun
fountain.**

22

The sun fountain is the happy, laughing heart of the garden. It is a literal fountain of youth as children stand, sit, and hurl themselves into it. Adults too seem to become younger at heart as they get a foot wet or laugh at children getting soaked.

Around the court are benches for adults to watch children play with the fountain and winds. A little toe or finger first greets the water, followed by a delighted squeal, which is quickly followed by a whole foot and hand feeling the water and then with an even louder squeal . . . and the fountain frolicker is soon happily soaked and laughing.

Surrounding the fountain are four boulders with storybook-like sculptures of the four winds, which "blow" a fine mist every few minutes, to the merry surprise of children. Look closely at each wind boulder to discover its carved seasonal images.

In the circular calendar that frames the court, find your birthday, the four solstice dates that mark the path of the sun, and even a crafty leap year figure stealing away a day in February. The circle of the year, the seasons, the sun, and the phases of the moon all reflect the cycle of a garden and the seed-to-seed cycle that supports all life.

The garden is filled with these kinds of subtle yet rich designs that visitors may not notice on the first visit.

The "blowing winds" catch children by surprise.

Going head to head with the autumn wind.

The waning and waxing phases of the moon are part of the fountain court's sundial. By standing below the moons, with their feet placed under the letter of the current month, children can tell the time by the shadow cast by their raised right hand. Each moon represents an hour from 8 a.m to 4 p.m., with the first moon on the left being 8 a.m. The full moon is high noon.

A Mulberry Fortress

Behind the fountain court rises a rolling hill with mighty mulberry fortresses. Six weeping mulberry trees with lush curtains of fountainous branches form a fantastic complex of forts and secret places perfect for hide and seek or just hiding.

Because the mulberries are male cultivars, they do not produce the blue-black fruits; they can concentrate their energy on producing those long, leafy branches

A green man in the children's garden peeks out of his mulberry tree fort.

that make such exquisite secret places for kids. Our apologies to the birds who love the fruits.

A grassy hilltop in front of the mulberry trees was created for toddlers to roll down and get happily dizzy.

Woodland

The natural, uncultivated world of plants is demonstrated in the garden's woodland area. Walking up a gentle slope from the fountain court, visitors pass under a grove of native serviceberry with underplantings of red twig dogwood, sweetspire, and oak leaf hydrangea shrubs. In early spring, the serviceberry lights up the woodland with a blizzard of white flowers. After flowering, these trees develop blue-black fruits beloved by birds.

The woodland area contains a number of beautiful specimen trees including Franklinia, Carolina silverbell, and redbuds. At its colorful peak in early spring, the redbud's intense pink and white flowers seem to hover in midair, attached to nothing but a beam of light streaming through the woodland.

In the summer, look for a grouping of old logs surrounding a soft bed of pine needles. Sit on the logs or lie down on the pine needles to enjoy the cool pine scent and shade of the serviceberries.

Running up into the shady native woodland.

Near the mulberry forts, visitors can rest or picnic on a tree-stump table and log chairs.

Walking along the woodland path, you'll pass under a Larch Arch. Look to your left to see Cotton Candy, a little pony that has wandered away from her pasture and shyly peeks out of the woods to see if any children might like to play with her. Cotton Candy is named for the pony Debra Hershey Guren wished for as a child. (While it took some time for the wish to come true, Debra finally did get a pony as a young woman and did indeed call her Cotton Candy.) Behind Cotton Candy are several specimen evergreens, including a concolor fir and a Serbian spruce that looks like a fat, laughing, coniferous Buddha.

A grove of white birch trees concludes the woodland area. The selection of white birch trees was inspired by "Birches," the Robert Frost poem about childhood and life's ups and downs.

The garden's pony, Cotton Candy, is reputed to help make wishes come true if they are whispered into her ear.

Prairie

Behind the formal Four Seasons Fountain Court is the native prairie meadow. The western Cleveland area represented the eastern edges of the Midwest prairies, and this planting pays homage to that unique natural heritage. Black-eyed Susan, purple coneflower, lupine,

Preparing for a meeting of the Hershey Children's Garden "young steering committee."

goldenrod, sunflower, shooting star, coreopsis, purple prairie clover, pink wild rose, prairie coneflower, Ohio spiderwort, and *Monardas* bloom brilliantly while June grass, little bluestem, prairie dropseed, and side oats grama grasses gently droop and wave in a breeze. Follow the stepping-stone path that cuts a swath through the meadow. Imagine more than two hundred years ago how prairie "oceans" stretched as far as the eye could see.

In the fall, the prairie grasses turn rich bronzy orange and wheat colors, creating a glowing warmth throughout the winter months.

Sometimes in late summer and fall, as plants sprawl over and go to seed, the prairie seems, to some visitors, neglected or too

The prairie's wild roses produce rosehips in late summer and fall.

Black-eyed Susan blooming in the Prairie Garden.

wild-looking to be "a garden." However, we purposely keep the area as natural as possible and do not deadhead flowers or cut back or stake plants, because the prairie is one of the ecological areas we use to educate visitors about natural ecosystems and native plants. This approach also rewards us with frequent sightings of goldfinches that love to eat the seeds of sunflowers and other plants.

We hope visitors are inspired to create their own backyard patches of prairie or other native plant species to help preserve these beautiful and important plants as well as to provide shelter and food for wildlife.

The treehouse towers over the garden like a child's castle.

Children carefully wade in the cool stream water with soft moss underfoot.

It's always an adventure to step from stone to stone to cross the pond.

Pond and Treehouse

The focal point of the entire garden, the treehouse looks like something out of a fable. Seen from the garden's entrance, it is like a child's dream of the ultimate treehouse.

This treehouse was designed to be accessible to all children, so visitors in wheelchairs can also enjoy the experience of being up in the treetops.

Along the path to the treehouse, a stream appears as if gently flowing down from a hill to empty into a pond. Rocks, boulders, grasses, and rushes planted along its edges create a

Walking along the pond's boardwalk, children brush against cattail plants.

29

Water lilies and lotus bloom near the pond bridge.

naturalistic effect. Sit on the bank and put your feet in the cool water.

Cross over the branch bridge or take the pond's boardwalk and stepping-stone path, brushing against cattails and grasses, to journey to the treehouse. Look for bright yellow flag iris in the spring and orange butterfly weed and flaming red cardinal flower in the summer. In early fall, milkweed releases its seed heads wrapped in a silky froth of fibers.

The pond is ever magnetic, beautiful, fascinating, and alive. All summer, the pond brings

A duck left his tracks as he waddled over to the bridge.

The sublime beauty of the pond's lotus flower in full bloom.

Monet's famous *Water Lilies* painting to life
as soft pink, white, and yellow hardy
water lilies float over half the pond. In
late summer, transcendent pearl pink
lotus flowers bloom and then reveal
smooth rattle-like seedpods as the petals
silently drop off.

Look and listen for the scores of
frogs that sit on the lilypads and croak
and ribbit all day. Hear the plunk . . .
plunk . . . plunk of frogs jumping from
the lilypads into the water as you pass by.
Watch the buzzing dragonflies skimming
the water and be on the lookout for
flashes of darting schools of goldfish.

**On any warm day, kids are on the dock
looking . . .**

and looking . . .

for goldfish.

All this action is best seen from the floating dock that juts into the pond from the treehouse area deck and gently bobs on the water like a boat. On any given day, you're guaranteed to see kids of all ages out on the dock—sitting, kneeling, and especially lying flat on their stomachs to get a better look at the goldfish flashing by in the depths. Kids giggle and shout when goldfish come along and tickle their toes or kiss their fingers as they swing feet and hands in the water.

It's also fun to watch water roll off lotus leaves like silver balls of mercury.

1, 2, 3, jump!

Behind the treehouse deck is a rock-climbing wall and a small cave for children to explore.

Climb up the rocks or stairs to reach the cooler treetop heights of the treehouse. Hold on to its smooth cedar railing and look out like a king or queen with a royal view of your garden realm. A perfect place for the imagination to soar, the treehouse is kept stocked with garden storybooks for children and families to read.

The treehouse is always stocked with garden and plant storybooks for children to read in a quiet place.

A bird's-eye view of the garden.

The treehouse is built around a nearly hundred-year-old tulip tree whose common name refers to its tulip-shaped leaves.

The Bird Garden
and Bird Blind

The bird garden is filled with a jumble of small native trees, shrubs, and perennials that attract birds by providing fruits or seeds for food, shelter for nesting, or materials for building nests.

As you leave the woodland, you'll come upon a hidden shelter surrounded by a thicket of shrubs. As you step inside this bird blind, peek through its many small windows to spy on colorful birds as they eat berries, sing, twitter, and build nests. You'll see and learn about goldfinches, cardinals, bluebirds, bluejays, robins, hummingbirds, and others common to northeast Ohio.

Getting a better look at a bird.

Bright red bunchberries and pink roses in the bird garden.

A bluejay decoy seen from the bird blind.

Birds love to snack on the garden's juicy serviceberries, sour rose hips, and jewel-like black clusters of elderberries. Giant sunflowers planted here and there in the shrubbery produce those fat, delicious seeds that birds (and squirrels) love so much. A birdbath provides water for bathing and drinking.

Can you find the old dead tree in the bird garden? Hollowed-out dead trees provide important shelters for birds and other wildlife.

The Dinosaur Garden

Near the bird garden is a dinosaur garden planted with several fossil plants—those that were around when the dinosaurs lived, many millennia ago.

The Grass Patch

Giant reed grass is the "magic bean" seed plant. Streaking to more than eighteen feet into the sky and dwarfing even giant sunflowers and some small trees, it is one of those extreme plants kids love. It seems to grow a foot or two when you turn your back on it even for a second. Like the mulberry tree forts, the grass patch is a place for nature to swallow kids whole and let them disappear from the world for a while.

Surrounding the "Giant" are a mix of miscanthus, zebra, and fountain grasses. Fountain grass's

When children are in the grass patch, we want them to feel like Jack, after he planted his magic bean seeds that grew sky high.

In addition to a mighty apatosaurus and stegosaurus, our dinosaur garden contains gingko trees, scouring rushes, and ferns—all ancient "fossil" plants.

35

fluffy soft plumes evoke delighted giggles as it tickles kids. Kids love to learn how the fountainous zebra grass got its name because of its green and yellow stripes that look like the colors of a zebra drawn by Dr. Seuss. On a windy day, the grass patch becomes a symphony of swishing sound.

The Cottage

The cottage is meant to evoke a storybook setting.

When we asked kids to draw what they'd like to have in a garden, many drew a little house with big flowers growing up around it. So, that is just what we created—a cottage surrounded by prairie flowers, not only around it but on top of it as well. As one of garden docents describes it, "It's not only *Little House on the Prairie* but also 'The Prairie on the Little House.'" By early summer, the roof is indeed a colorful patch of coreopsis, gaillardia, black-eyed Susan, and fescue grasses. Many visitors ask how we plant the roof. The wildflower roof is "planted" every spring, in mid-April, with specially ordered wildflower sod. Just like regular turf sod, it arrives looking like a big seaweed sushi roll or carpet roll. It is unrolled, cut to measure, pressed on top of the four-inch-deep soil, and kept well watered.

Kids love to pretend it's their own little house. Most of all, they seem to love going into the cottage, closing the window shutters and door, and screaming because they are in the dark! A children's garden just can't have enough of these little secret places! Inside the cottage are a pint-sized table and chairs along with several kid-sized brooms.

Children love the child-sized brooms we keep in the garden. They like to sweep with them . . .

. . . and "fly" on them . . .

. . . and because the brooms proved to be so popular with kids, we planted a "broom garden" to show them how brooms have been traditionally crafted from broom corn. A giant Harry Potter–type broomstick underscores the lesson in a playful way.

Kids get dizzy running around and around in the maze.

The Maze

A classic garden feature loved (and sometimes feared) by all ages is a maze. Set between the Four Seasons Fountain Court and the Scrounger's Garden, the maze nicely separates these two busy and colorful areas and serves as a soothingly all-green resting place for the eyes.

Soft-scaled arborvitae evergreens were planted close together in a spiral pattern. Yet another place where kids can hide, the maze adds fun and mystery to the garden. What *is* in the center?

In fall, the flowering crabapple cultivar 'Lancelot' at the center of the maze is covered in gorgeous golden yellow fruits.

Kids enter and exit under child-sized arbors. On reaching the center, they find a Goldilocks woodland bench—one that's not too big and not too small, but just right.

The Vegetable Patch

An important objective of the garden is to educate children about where food comes from. Our edible-plant areas aim to teach kids that it is gardens, not grocery stores, that produce carrots, corn, potatoes, tomatoes, apples, and more— indeed, everything we eat, because all food comes directly or indirectly from plants.

Charming carrot gates usher visitors into the vegetable patch.

To make a vegetable garden interesting for kids, we plan different planting themes and layouts each season, ranging from educational to fun and silly.

To keep it playful, we've grown a Peter Rabbit Garden with all the garden plants Peter loved to eat and a Sun Garden with yellow beans, yellow tomatoes, yellow peppers, golden zucchini, and yellow nasturtiums. Once children learn they can eat the peppery nasturtium leaf, most love to take a taste each time they visit the garden.

To join in the excitement of the real Olympic games, one summer we hosted our own "Bean Olympics" that

Carrot gates lead into the vegetable and herb gardens.

Tasty lettuces and carrots grow in the Peter Rabbit Garden.

After cooling
down in the
fountain, a
young visitor
picks a sweet
cherry tomato.

pitted three climbing beans against one another. Gold, silver, and bronze medals were awarded in accordance with when each bean cultivar reached the top of an eight-foot pole.

One spring, we had children spell out the words *salad bar* with a rainbow of garden greens seeds. We've planted Vincent Van Gogh's sunflower garden filled with a variety of sunflowers to show children where sunflower seeds come from and how this beautiful flower inspired a great artist.

We've planted a "Three Sisters" squash, bean, and corn garden for kids to learn the beautiful Native American story of how the three plants are close friends who help each other. Corn allows bean to grow up her stalk, bean returns the favor by enriching the soil for corn and squash, and squash spreads her leaves over the ground near bean and squash to keep the soil moist and weeds away.

Whatever the theme, from spring's spicy arugula greens and radishes, to summer's sugary cherry tomatoes and crisp peppers and fall's grapes, there is always something edible for kids to see and taste.

Orchard and Berry Patch

Dwarf apple, pear, and cherry trees, along with strawberries, raspberries, and grapes, grow in this jungly and juicy Berry Patch. Like the vegetable patch, The Berry Patch allows children to see how these fruits grow and to pick and taste these delicious fruits "straight out the garden."

Children are welcome to pick ripe raspberries anytime in The Berry Patch.

40

The Berry Patch also demonstrates to visitors how an abundance of different fruits can be grown in a small area. Wasting no space but adding an interesting effect, two espaliered fruit trees (one apple and one pear) serve as a living fence around The Berry Patch.

Children's Herb Garden

With its snaking cobblestone path that winds under living willow arbors entwined with purple morning glories and leads to a garden throne, this is a seriously cute herb garden. It is filled with plants like chocolate mint, peppermint, and lemon balm that kids love to discover and taste. Kids also see, taste, and learn about oregano, basil, parsley, and marjoram, the "pizza herbs" that make the sauce on those pies taste so good.

Garden docents encourage kids to discover the scents of lavender, sweet Annie, and rosemary and show them how to rub the leaves of pineapple sage

Sniffing verbena in the herb garden near living willow arbors covered by purple morning glories.

between their fingers to release its delicious pineapple scent. Clumps of catnip are grown so kids can pick a stem and take home a special treat for their kitty.

A "Smell This Plant" sign placed near a rosemary plant in the herb garden lets visitors know to savor the scent of this wonderfully fragrant herb.

In addition to investigating the root-view cabinets in the garden, children can also lift up water hyacinths from a water garden container to see how the roots of this water plant grow.

Root-View Cabinets

Roots are the hard-working, behind- and below-the-scenes plant parts that are underappreciated because they go unseen. The garden's root-view cabinet allows children to see roots and learn how they support plants.

Compost Bins

Hershey Children's Garden has a three-bin compost system: one for fresh material, a middle one for

"cooking" the plant material to speed decomposition, and a third to hold the finished compost until it is ready to be added to garden beds to enrich the soil. Removable front boards allow the bin height to be adjusted to make it easier for kids to add or remove compost.

We invite kids to pull a weed or a faded flower and toss it into the compost bin. Kids learn by "recycling" such items as weeds, flowers, fruit, and grass clippings that they will decompose and become "garden food."

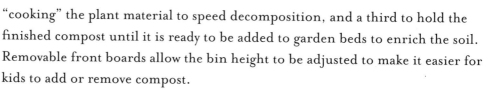

Kids love to help us sift material from the finished compost bin before it is added to the garden. We place a screen over a wheelbarrow and kids use trowels to scoop the finished compost onto it to sift out the larger pieces. When the wheelbarrow is full, kids help us empty out this "black gold" into flower, vegetable, and woodland beds.

Scrounger's Garden

What if children who visit the garden live in the city with no growing space or in an apartment without any yard space? How can they have a garden?

Our Scrounger's Garden was designed to be a fun and whimsical garden space that also demonstrates how any child can have a little garden—even if they have only a windowsill, a balcony, or a tiny yard.

The Scrounger's Garden scrounges items normally thrown away to demonstrate how a garden doesn't have to cost a lot. An old shoe, boot, teakettle, saucepan, basket, coffee can, seashell, filing cabinet, bathtub, and drainpipes all can be filled with soil and planted with flowers, herbs, and even vegetables!

A Scrounger's Garden has a fun-loving soul fueled by creativity and the thrifty desire to reclaim, recycle, and reinvent. An old bicycle wheel becomes a crown for the top of a vine pole; an old cowboy boot becomes a birdhouse; an old metal rake becomes a branch for birds; a silver soupspoon becomes a dragonfly; and a filing cabinet becomes a planter.

A recycled spider web with eyeglass-lens "dewdrops."

Every garden needs impatiens planted in a polka-dot shoe.

Containers for our Scrounger's Garden are scrounged from thrift stores, flea markets, yard sales and spring-cleaned garages, attics, basements, kitchens, closets, and cars.

As long as an object can hold some soil and drain water, it is eligible for Scrounger-hood. However, while drainage potential will get an object in the scrounger door, it must also have charm, personality, and wit to ultimately make the Scrounger grade.

Once you "get" the Scrounger mentality, instead of reaching for yet another terra-cotta pot, you'll use an empty olive oil can or fireman's boot instead. What can you find that could make the Scrounger grade?

The recyled tin man "waters" recycled "flowers" in the Scounger's Garden.

A yellow wheelbarrow hauls a load of white petunias in the Scrounger's Garden.

44

Water, Water Everywhere . . .

Adjacent to the Scrounger's Garden are three hand pumps for visitors to use as a drinking fountain and especially for kids to fill watering cans to water plants in the Scrounger's Garden.

In June 1999, before the garden opened to the public, we were in the middle of exceptionally hot weather and a drought. With dozens of Scrounger containers that dried out easily, I worried how we would keep up with the watering all day long.

Happily, on opening day, children immediately filled watering cans and made beelines to the Scrounger's Garden to water all the containers. Our problem turned from drought to deluge. We joke that water lilies would probably grow better in the Scrounger's Garden than in the pond.

Digging Pit

So much of gardening is about digging and playing in the dirt. The digging pit lets little ones practice their digging skills—especially how to get nice and dirty—for when they grow up to be gardeners someday.

Let the temperature soar and droughts persist—teapots, purses, and plants in our Scrounger's Garden never go thirsty.

Sometimes it takes a while to figure things out.

A log border encloses the digging pit while across the way, upended wine bottles edge part of the Scrounger's Garden.

Future gardener at work.

International Garden

Because Cleveland is a melting pot of ethnic groups, we created an International Garden to celebrate this rich heritage by showcasing plants native to or closely associated with North and South America, Asia, Europe and the Mediterranean, the Middle East, and Africa.

In Asia, kids can see what a banana tree looks like and in South America, they learn where tomatoes, corn, and marigolds originated. North America displays its beautiful native plants that attract butterflies, including Joe-Pye weed, black-eyed Susan, and butterfly weed.

A garden gnome stands guard in "Europe."

Walking by Europe in the spring, kids see bright red tulips associated with the Netherlands.

46

The Mediterranean and Middle East are the most fragrant parts of the "world" with their abundance of aromatic herbs including lavender, oregano, thyme, sage, patchouli, and curry plants.

Passing by Africa, kids will see gourds growing up tripod trellises, spiky yuccas, brilliant scarlet crocosmia, and bright golden yellow osteospermum flowers, all native to that continent.

Mud Pie Mondays and Cider Sundays

From spring egg hunts to summer mud pies and fall scarecrow festivals, Hershey Children's Garden celebrates every season with fun activities and events for visitors.

Making color-ful mud pies on a summer Monday morning.

Every Sunday in October, children can help us make and sample fresh apple cider.

47

Dancing with the scarecrows during the annual Scarecrow Festival in the children's garden.

Tagging monarch butterflies as part of a research project on monarch migration.

A Place to Grow

Since the Hershey Children's Garden opened, thousands of children and adults have visited. Our hope is that this garden touches the hearts and minds of children today so that, one day, they come back to the garden with their children and grandchildren because they want them to experience its magic and discoveries as they did as children.

We hope the garden plants the seed for children to become passionate gardeners and environmental advocates who create their own magical gardens and protect natural spaces as they grow.

Acknowledgments

Everyone involved in this project poured mind and heart into creating an amazing children's garden. As in the stone soup story, when we began to dream of the kind of garden we wanted, people started to appear with the funds, talents, and skills to help create the garden we envisioned.

We are so thankful for their hard work and the excellence they demonstrated in creating the garden.

Major Garden Donors:

Jo Hershey Selden Charitable Remainder Trust
The Hershey Foundation and members of the Hershey family

Garden Designer:

Herb Schaal, EDAW

Garden Planning Committee:

Debra Hershey Guren, Trustee
Brian Holley, Executive Director
Maureen Heffernan, Director of Public Programs
Young-Mi Moon, Hershey Children's Garden Manager
Mark Druckenbrod, Director of Research and Conservation
Paul Pfeifer and Larry Giblock, Horticulturists
Ruth Moorhead, Trustee

Donley Construction Company: Andrew Wasiniak, Project Manager
Peter Baumgartner, construction foreman

Jeff Knopp, landscape architect, Benhke & Associates

Others:

Ken Roby, blacksmith, Auburn, Ohio
Roger Gettig, from the Holden Arboretum in Kirtland, Ohio, helped select plants for the prairie meadow.
Hannah Wendick-Mason, Hershey Children's Garden manager, 2001–2003
Kyle Bradford, Hershey Children's Garden intern, 1999–2004

Visitor Information

Hershey Children's Garden is located at Cleveland Botanical Garden.

In the heart of University Circle, Cleveland's cultural center, the Garden features ten acres of display gardens and the Eleanor Armstrong Smith Glasshouse.

The Garden is located at 11030 East Boulevard in Cleveland, Ohio.

For more information on our gardens, exhibits, events, tickets, hours of operation, and driving directions, please visit: www.cbgarden.org.

The Photographers

Ian Adams is an environmental photographer specializing in natural, historical, rural, and garden landscapes. More than 2,500 of his photographs have been published in books, calendars, posters, magazines, and other publications. For more information, visit Ian's website: *www.ianadamsphotography.com.*

Dixi Carrillo is a professional photographer from Colorado Springs, Colorado, who has documented gardens designed by EDAW landscape architects.

Janet Century is a Cleveland-area photographer whose photographs for the book, *A Walk in the Park,* showcased Greater Cleveland's parks, gardens, and other greenspaces.

Sara Guren, a native Clevelander, has studied photography at Rocky Mountain School of Photography in Missoula, Montana. As a documentary photographer, Sara works with horses, dogs, people, and children. She can be reached through her website at www.saraguren.com.

Photo credits:

Ian Adams: pages x, 1, 5, 12 (bottom left and right), 13 (top), 15, 21 (top and middle), 27 (top), 28, 30, 34 (bottom left), 44, back cover

Dixi Carrillo: pages 23, 38 (top)

Janet Century: pages v, xii, 2, 3, 12 (top), 13 (bottom), 14, 16, 17, 19, 20, 21 (bottom), 22 (top), 24 (top), 25 (top), 26 (bottom), 27, 29, 31, 32, 33 (bottom left), 34 (top and right), 35, 37, 38 (bottom), 39 (top), 40, 41 (top right), 42 (bottom), 43, 46 (bottom), 47, 48, front cover

Sara Guren: pages ii, viii, 22 (bottom), 24 (bottom), 25 (bottom), 26 (top), 33 (bottom right), 36, 41 (bottom left), 42 (top), 45, 46 (top left and right), 49

Art on first page and page 7 by Caroline Gray

Photographs not otherwise credited are property of Cleveland Botanical Garden or the author.